The Weather Forecast

Written and Illustrated by
John Ryan

One day Mr Noah called all the Ark family into his room. 'Just look at the weather house,' he cried. 'The fine-weather man is further out than ever before. It's going to be a really beautiful day today!'

So everybody gathered round to see. They all knew
about the weather house. When it was going to rain
a lady with an umbrella came out of one of the doors.
And when it was going to be fine a smiling fine-
weather man came out of the other. There he was.
Anyone could see that today it was going to be fine.

'In that case,' said Mrs Noah, 'I shall do the washing. It will be a good drying day.' 'The paintwork could do with some touching up,' said cheerful Ham. 'I'll see to that!'

Even gloomy Mr and
Mrs Shem looked quite
cheerful. 'I'll scrub the deck
and you polish the brass-
work,' said Shem to his wife.

'And I shall make some good, fresh lemonade,' said
Mrs Ham. 'We shall all be thirsty on a fine hot day
like this.' Only Mr Noah's youngest son Jaffet and his
friend Jannet didn't seem too happy,

because when they looked
out of the window the
weather didn't look fine at
all.

There were big, black clouds rolling up all over the
horizon. And there was something else that worried them.

The two dormice were missing from among the Ark
animals. Jaffet and Jannet and Crockle their pet
baby crocodile had spent all day looking for them.

'Never mind about the weather,' said Jaffet. 'We must find them!' 'Maybe they've been gobbled up by one of the big cats,' said Jannet. 'They've been looking very hungry lately.'

'So have the crocodiles,' said Jaffet.

'A boa constrictor might have swallowed them . . . or a hippo might have trampled on them,' said Jaffet. 'How awful!' cried Jannet. 'We'll have to tell Mr Noah.'

But Mr Noah was far more
interested in the weather
than in any missing
dormice.

Can't you
see I'm busy?

'I tell you what,' he said, 'Take the animals you
suspect out on deck and ask them about the dormice.
The fresh air will be good for them anyway.'

Outside on deck everybody was hard at work, washing and painting and scrubbing and polishing. The clouds were blacker than ever, but everybody believed Mr Noah's weather forecast. Mrs Ham was just handing round the lemonade

when Jaffet and Jannet arrived with a pair of tigers.

But when they asked them

> Do you know anything about two little lost dormice?

the tigers shook their heads. So did the lions and the leopards and all the other big cats.

The crocodiles shed several large crocodile tears when they heard about the dormice, but they shook their heads too.

And so did the boa constrictors. All this time the sky was getting darker and darker. Jaffet and Jannet had just arrived with the two hippos, when suddenly

there was a bright flash of lightning and a loud clap of thunder!

And a few moments later

a great wave struck the Ark
and knocked it sideways.

And that was the end of all the hard work on deck.
The paint went all over the two hippos.

The lemonade went all over Mrs Noah, who very
nearly fell overboard.

Mr and Mrs Shem lost their footing and slid all over the deck,

and Mr Noah did somersaults from one side of the Ark to the other.

It looked as though Mr Noah's weather house had got the weather forecast all wrong.

By now one of the hippos was striped like a zebra,

and the other had spots like a leopard, only they were red.

Mr Noah was stuck upside-
down in the doorway

and Mrs Noah was clinging
to the washing line.

Mr and Mrs Shem were covered with wet washing
and Ham had a bucket on his head.

Then Ham shouted:

'Come on everybody!
Under cover before the next
big wave!' So they all picked
themselves up and ran indoors.

The thunderstorm went on. When the children got the two hippos down below they found all the animals very frightened. The bigger they were the more they were alarmed by the flashes and the crashes of the storm.

The children had quite a job calming the lions down.

There there

HOWL HOWL

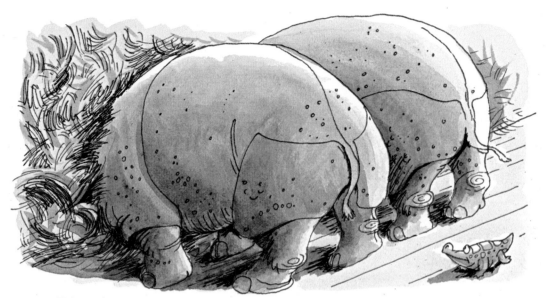

The rhinos hid their heads in the straw and pretended they weren't there at all

and the elephants kept their trunks crossed and hoped for the best.

Then the huge waves struck again. Higher and
higher they came

and as the ship was tossed this way and that only the
sea-birds from the Ark seemed safe and happy.

Inside, the animals started to slide up and down in a great howling, roaring, squealing heap. The heavy elephants hung on with their trunks so as to stop squashing the others,

and the rhinos and the hippos managed to wedge themselves at either end so as to make themselves into enormous cushions. Even so, it was very dangerous for the smaller animals with so many huge bodies flying to and fro.

So Jaffet and Jannet
collected them together

and tucked them away in
safe places like a pair of old
gumboots

and chests of drawers and
mugs and barrels. For an
hour or more the terrible
storm raged.

Then, almost as suddenly as it had started, it began to die away. The wind dropped, the rain stopped and the sun came out from behind the clouds. The water became calmer and calmer,

and quite soon the Ark was on an even keel again.

Everybody began to feel better.

Even though they had felt seasick, Mr and Mrs Ham set to work again to scrub and polish, and Mrs Noah made a fresh start with the washing. Ham found some new paint for the doors and windows,

and Mrs Ham began to cut up fresh lemons to make lemonade.

There was so much for Jaffet and Jannet to do that they forgot about the two dormice who were still missing. Some of the animals needed first aid,

and the hippos had to have their spots and stripes
scrubbed off.

Then, when everything was finished, the two children
went off to report to Mr Noah.

But they found Mr Noah was very cross because his weather house had got the weather forecast all wrong.

'It's a rotten useless thing,' he said. 'I shall throw it away!'

And he took it down from the wall and tossed it on to the floor.

But just as Jaffet went to pick it up and throw it overboard, Crockle started to sniff at the weather house.

He sniffed and sniffed and sniffed so hard that the children bent down to have a really good look. There was a hole in the back, and what should they find inside

but the two missing dormice, in a snug little nest.

Mr Noah was delighted. 'Why of *course*,' he cried, 'that's why my weather house was wrong. The fine-weather man was pushed out of the door when the dormice built their nest . . . and *he couldn't get in again*.'

And he gently took the dormice out and proudly hung up his weather house again. 'There,' he said. 'I knew it was a good weather forecaster really.
'In fact I don't know *what* we should do without it!'

'Well!' said Jaffet. 'We'd have thrown both the weather house and, far worse, the two dormice overboard if it hadn't been for Crockle!

'I don't know what we'd do
without *him*!'